The World's Funniest Roast Jokes

The World's Funniest Roast Jokes

for hilarious parties and events

By Red Stangland

Meadowbrook Press
Distributed by Simon & Schuster
New York

Library of Congress Cataloging-in-Publication Data

Stangland, E.C.
    The world's funniest roast jokes / by Red Stangland.
        p.   cm.
    ISBN: 0-88166-187-2
    1. Roasts (Public speaking) 2. Wit and humor. I. Title.
PN4193.R63S73 1992
808.5'1—dc20

92-6367
CIP

S & S Ordering #: 0-671-78051-4

Editor: Bruce Lansky
Copy Editor: Elizabeth H. Weiss
Proofreader: Jay Johnson
Production Manager: Lynne Cromwell
Production Assistant: Matthew Thurber
Typographer: Jon C. Wright
Cover Art: Nathan Jarvis
Text Design: Tabor Harlow

© 1992 by Red Stangland

Published by Meadowbrook Press, 18318 Minnetonka Boulevard, Deephaven, MN 55391.

BOOK TRADE DISTRIBUTION by Simon & Schuster, a division of Simon and Schuster, Inc., 1230 Avenue of the Americas, New York, NY 10020.

97 96 95 94 93 92   6 5 4 3 2 1

Printed in the United States of America

DEDICATION WITH THANKS

To my good friend Henny Youngman, "King of the One-Liners," who took me behind the scenes at Friar's roasts in New York and Hollywood; to Paul Olson, owner of KLEN, LeMars, Iowa, for his great roast joke collection; and to Bruce Lansky of Meadowbrook Press for his editing genius.

CONTENTS

Lifestyle

Personality

Profession

Religion and Nationality

Sex Life

Endings

INTRODUCTION

Imagine having a famous comedian like Bob Hope, Henny Youngman, or Milton Berle at your next family reunion, company gathering, or community event. By deftly toasting and roasting the guest of honor (to the delight of all in attendance), any one of these noted comics could turn a run-of-the-mill party into a hilarious occasion.

But since you might have to sell your house to pay for such high-caliber talent, we have the next best thing: the collected witticisms of the best roast masters in the United States. I have attended several Friar's Club Roasts as the guest of Henny Youngman, and with my own private stock of roast jokes, I have assembled the brightest, most hilarious collection of roast gags you'll find anywhere. I have watched the comic greats—Rich Little, Norm Crosby, Buddy Hackett, Milton Berle, Henny Youngman, and many more—at star-studded roasts in New York and Hollywood as they matched wits with the biggest names in Show Biz.

As a joke publisher, I have sold over a million books that have set people laughing from coast to coast. And now, I have made it easy to roast *your* guest of honor like a pro. The jokes in this book are organized by topic. All you have to do is consult the Contents for the personality traits you wish to focus on while roasting the guest of honor. This book will let you come on like a seasoned comedian and zing your "victim" with the greatest of ease. The roastee will love it; the audience will howl with delight. And planning with *The World's Funniest Roast Jokes* will ensure the success of your party or event.

A Word about Roast Jokes

Roast jokes or "zingers" are one-liners that poke fun at someone, using some aspect of the roastee's personality, appearance, behavior, religion, or lifestyle as a point of departure. There's no need to strive for journalistic accuracy when choosing and delivering the jokes—often the further afield you go, the better. Although you might think that it's embarassing to be the butt of roast jokes, the humorous attention actually comes across as complimentary and flattering. Believe me, it's as much fun to be roasted as it is to do the roasting!

How to Create a Roast Routine:

1. Decide which of the guest of honor's traits will provide good roast material. If you are throwing an "over-the-hill" party, you might turn to "Old" in the Appearance section and choose appropriate jokes about aging. Take it a step further by choosing jokes that are more specific. For example, if your guest of honor is a Jewish lawyer who loves to play golf, you'll find hilarious material in the Religion and Nationality, Profession, and Lifestyle sections, respectively. You can even set up the jokes to reflect the *opposite* of what makes the guest of honor special—use jokes from "Unfashionable" to make fun of an impeccable dresser or jokes from "Dishonest" to kid your church official. Both methods are sure to get a laugh!

2. Check off the jokes that you think are funny in the little box in the upper left-hand corner of each roast joke.

3. Photocopy the pages you plan to use.

4. Customize the jokes by filling each blank with the guest of honor's name and appropriate pronouns.

5. Circle the specific jokes you want to use, or cut out each joke along the dotted lines provided.

6. Number the jokes, and put them in order so your presentation tells a story or comes off as a real comedy routine.

7. Use the jokes as reminder cards, holding them in your hand and reading them aloud one by one. Or tape them onto a large sheet of paper, in order, so they're easy to read. If you really want to get adventurous, you can memorize the jokes like a true stand-up comic.

How to Host a Roast:

1. If there will be more than one "roaster," decide who will do the toasts,

introductions, and roast jokes, and provide them with copies of the chosen material. You can create the routines yourself or give a copy of this book to the other hosts and let them get creative.

2. If the roast isn't intended as a surprise, it's only fair to provide the guest of honor with copies of comebacks and roast jokes he or she can use in rebuttal. (Again, you can either create the rebuttal routine or let the guest of honor create it.)

3. Make sure you have a good sound system for your roast.

About sound systems:

- For large gatherings, one microphone at the speaker's stand is usually sufficient.

- If you want to emulate a TV or club roast, rent a convention room from a hotel, and request a dais with a raised speaker's stand and two microphones; one for the roaster and the other for the guest of honor.

- For informal parties at home, you won't need a sound system. You can hold a roast around your dining room table, in the living room, or even in the backyard.

Note: A roast is not only a great way to add humor to an otherwise dull event— it's also a good way to raise money for your favorite charity. Most people will pay to attend a roast featuring a prominent guest of honor and notable roasters.

How to Host a Roast Party

A roast is a fun and easy way to turn any small gathering into a laugh riot. Here's how to do it:

1. Have one person hold the book and read a customized roast joke about any other person in the group.

2. Pass the book to the roastee, and have him or her read one rebuttal joke about the person who has just roasted him or her, and one *new* roast joke to someone else in the group.

3. Continue roasting in this manner until everyone in the group has roasted and been roasted several times and is too tired to laugh anymore.

Other Uses for Roast Jokes

Test some roast jokes at the next convention or civic gathering, birthday party, or anniversary celebration you host or attend. Or take this book to work and roast your boss or co-workers during a coffee break. No matter where you use it, this book will inspire every reader to stand up and be comic!

There's always room for a few more of the world's best roast jokes. I'd love to hear from you if you've come across a roast joke or idea that would enhance this book. Write to me at: Box 1554, Sioux Falls, SD 57101.

Happy roasting!

Red Stangland

Beginnings

TOASTS

❑

Here's to a _____ who offers living
(man/woman)
proof that only the good die young.

❑

Here's to a _____ I can't praise
(man/woman)
enough—considering _____ close
(his/her)
connection to the Mafia.

❑

Here's to our poor friend, _____. The first
(Name)
half of _____ life was ruined by _____
(his/her)   (his/her)
parents. And the second half was ruined by
_____ kids.
(his/her)

❑

I'd like to toast this very kind _____
(man/woman)
who *always* has time for _____ friends—
(his/her)
_____ loves to show off _____
(he/she)   (his/her)
_____.
(Rolex/Timex)

❑

I'd like to propose a toast to a _____
(man/woman)
with a soft heart, and a head to match.

❑

Let's raise our glasses high to a _____
(man/woman)
who has the highest reputation for integrity
that money can buy.

❑

Here's a toast to a carefree _____.
(man/woman)
_____ doesn't care what happens—as
(Name)
long as it happens to somebody else.

❑

I'd like to propose a toast to a _____
(man/woman)
who's been called rude, arrogant, and self-
centered. But that's just the opinion of
_____ friends.
(his/her)

INTRODUCTIONS

❏

I didn't come here to bore you with a long speech. I can do it just as well with a short one.

❏

It's always a pleasure to introduce a dear friend. But instead, I have to introduce _____ .
(Name)

❏

Tonight's guest needs no introduction. What _____ needs is a conclusion.
(he/she)

❏

I'll never forget the first time I met _____
(Name)
—but I'm trying.

❏

I'd like to introduce an energetic and exciting speaker. But today our guest of honor is _____ .
(Name)

❏

There will be some people here tonight who will say that _____ is a _____ of
(Name)   (man/woman)
the highest integrity—and there will be those who will tell the truth.

❏

_____ is quite modest. And I must say,
(Name)
_____ has a great deal to be modest
(he/she)
about.

❏

_____ , I looked high and low for you.
(Name)
I just didn't look low enough.

INTRODUCTIONS

❑

It's a pleasure to introduce _____—a
                                (Name)
_____ I could never recommend too
(man/woman)
highly. Come to think of it, I can't recom-

mend _____ at all.
        (him/her)

❑

_____ , you don't seem to be yourself
(Name)
lately, and I noticed the improvement.

❑

Our guest of honor has earned every bit of

_____ success the old-fashioned way—
(his/her)
bribery, blackmail, and extortion.

❑

It's a pleasure to introduce a _____
                               (man/woman)
who couldn't have done a better job for

_____ if _____ had tried.
(Company/Organization)   (he/she)
So _____ didn't try.
    (he/she)

❑

I'd like to introduce a _____ who
                        (man/woman)
always leaves you with a good feeling. It's

like the good feeling you get when you stop

knocking your head against a wall.

❑

There are a lot of people who believe in you,

_____ . But there are a lot of people who
(Name)
believe in the Easter Bunny, too.

❑

I'd like to introduce a _____ with
                        (man/woman)
no equals—only superiors.

❑

I'd like to introduce a _____ who's
                        (man/woman)
been like a _____ to me—rude,
             (son/daughter)
obnoxious, and ungrateful.

RESPONSES TO INTRODUCTIONS

❑

It's always difficult to follow an outstanding speaker. Fortunately, I don't have that problem tonight.

❑

Thank you,_____, for that introduction.
(Name)
What you lacked in clarity and wit, you certainly made up for in length.

❑

I've been introduced many times in many ways, but your introduction of me tonight, _____, was certainly the most recent.
(Name)

❑

_____, it's always a pleasure to be
(Name)
introduced by an entertaining speaker. But this just isn't my lucky day.

Appearance

OLD

❑

I don't want you to get the idea that_____
(Name)
is old, but when they lit the candles on

_____ last birthday cake, the smoke
(his/her)
alarm went off.

❑

_____ tells me that the only places he can
(Name)
grow hair anymore are his nose and ears.

❑

_____'s doctor told _____ recently,
(Name)   (him/her)
"At your age, you could go at anytime."

_____ answered, "I'm glad to hear that
(Name)
because I haven't gone for days."

❑

_____ is so old that when _____ goes
(Name)   (he/she)
to a restaurant and orders a three-minute

egg, they make _____ pay in advance.
(him/her)

❑

We all know _____ is old, but don't
(Name)
believe the rumor that_____was a waiter
(he/she)
at the Last Supper.

❑

_____ is at the age when _____has all
(Name)   (he/she)
the answers. Trouble is—nobody asks

_____ any questions.
(him/her)

❑

I don't know for sure how old_____is,
(Name)
but he was circumcised with a stone knife.

❑

I read in a history book that it was our guest

of honor, _____, who told Betsy Ross,
(Name)
"Personally I think that pattern is a little

busy—but let's run it up the flagpole, and see

if anyone salutes."

OLD

❑

_____ is at that stage in life when
(Name)
_____ mind says *go* and _____ body
(his/her)   (his/her)
says *no!*

❑

_____ is so old that _____ not only has
(Name)   (he/she)
to give up smoking but also what comes

before it.

❑

Sex at _____'s age is like shooting pool
(Name)
with a rope.

❑

_____ says _____ feels like a twenty
(Name)   (he/she)
year old but can't find one who'll go out with

_____ .
(him/her)

❑

_____ is in that glorious period of life
(Name)
known as "middle age"—when you go from

stud to dud.

❑

_____ is at an age when the only reason
(Name)
for sailing on the *Love Boat* is to play

shuffleboard.

❑

_____'s kids were looking at an old
(Name)
family photo album the other night and came

across a picture of _____ when _____
(Name)   (he/she)
was much younger. The kids asked, "Who *is*

this?" Their _____ replied, "That's
(mother/father)
your _____ ." The kids exclaimed,
(father/mother)
"Then who the heck is the old geezer living

with us?"

OVERWEIGHT

❑

_____'s doctor has a digital scale in his
(Name)
office. When_____steps on the scale, it
(Name)
reads: "One at a time, please."

❑

_____ was once so overweight that when
(Name)
a doctor tried to take a blood sample, he got
gravy.

❑

The doctor told _____ that if _____
(Name)   (he/she)
wanted to lose weight, _____ should ride
(he/she)
a horse. The very first week, the horse lost
ten pounds.

❑

I recently saw_____ wearing a T-shirt
(Name)
with the message: "Life is uncertain. Eat
dessert first."

SMELLY

❑

_____'s breath is so bad, the dentist
(Name)
gave _____ a root canal through
(him/her)
_____ ears.
(his/her)

❑

_____ is quite well known nationally—
(Name)
_____ was the poster child for B.O.
(he/she)

❑

Anyone who thinks _____has run out of
(Name)
gas should join _____ some night for a
(him/her)
few bowls of Mexican chili.

❑

Did you hear that the President has released
his clean-air act? It has three basic parts:
Reduce sulphur emissions; increase use of
ethanol fuels; and order_____to change
(Name)
_____ socks more often.
(his/her)

UGLY (AS AN ADULT)

❏

When _____ went out to Hollywood last
_(Name)
month, a lot of people said he looks just like

a movie star—Harpo Marx.

❏

_____ has bedroom eyes—a pillow
_(Name)
under each one.

❏

_____ went to the dentist and asked,
_(Name)
"Doc, what should I do about my yellow

teeth?" The dentist said, "Wear brown."

❏

_____ went to the beauty shop yesterday
_(Name)
and stayed two hours. And that was just for

the *estimate.*

❏

_____ was telling me that _____
_(Name) _(he/she)
couldn't find anyone to go out with. I said,

"_____, what you need is a blind date—
_(Name)
and I do mean *blind.*"

❏

You could say _____ looks like a million
_(Name)
bucks—green and wrinkled.

❏

When _____ went to the doctor to get
_(Name)
_____ , the doctor said,
_(a vasectomy/birth control pills)
"With your looks, I wouldn't bother."

❏

_____ got _____ good looks from
_(Name) _(his/her)
_____ father. He's a plastic surgeon.
_(his/her)

UGLY (AS A CHILD)

☐

_____was so ugly at birth, the doctor
(Name)
slapped _____ mother.
(his/her)

☐

_____ was such an ugly baby, the nurses
(Name)
diapered _____ face.
(his/her)

☐

You want to know how ugly_____was?
(Name)
_____ parents were so embarrassed they
(His/Her)
borrowed another baby for the baptism
ceremony.

☐

In school,_____was teacher's pet—the
(Name)
teacher couldn't afford a dog.

UNFASHIONABLE

☐

_____ , you dress beautifully for
(Name)
someone who's color blind.

☐

I like that outfit you're wearing,_____ .
(Name)
You should hang on to it—it might come
back in style someday.

☐

Say, _____ , that's a nice suit you're
(Name)
wearing. When did the clown die?

☐

After seeing your outfit, _____ , I get the
(Name)
feeling that somewhere in this town there's a
horse that's getting cold.

UNFASHIONABLE

❏

_____, I love that jacket you're
(Name)
wearing—it's clear you shop at only the
finest garage sales.

❏

_____, I love that suit you're wearing.
(Name)
You never throw anything away, do you?

❏

_____, I really wish you'd do something
(Name)
about the way you dress. I mean, every time
you walk into a room someone yells, "Who
called a cab?"

❏

_____ wears unusual clothes. His tie has
(Name)
the Italian look—it has wine stains all over it.

Behavior

CHEAP

❑

Did you hear that last month_____'s
(Name)
_____ had _____ MasterCard
(wife/husband)   (her/his)
stolen? But_____ doesn't mind—the thief
(Name)
is charging less than _____ _____ .
(his/her)   (wife/husband)

❑

_____ is ambidextrous—_____ can't
(Name)   (he/she)
find _____ billfold with both hands.
(his/her)

❑

I found out how slow-motion pictures were
invented—someone filmed _____ picking
(Name)
up the check in a restaurant.

❑

The last time _____ picked up the dinner
(Name)
check was at McDonald's.

❑

You can always recognize _____in a
(Name)
restaurant. _____ the one sitting with
(He's/She's)
_____ back to the check.
(his/her)

❑

_____ says _____doesn't stay at the
(Name)   (he/she)
Holiday Inn anymore because the towels are
so thick it's too hard to close _____
(his/her)
suitcase.

❑

_____ is always complaining about how
(Name)
prices are going up. I told _____ that it
(him/her)
just seems that way because it's been so
long since _____ paid for anything.
(he/she)

❑

_____ is so cheap that _____went on
(Name)   (he/she)
_____ honeymoon alone.
(his/her)

CHEAP

❏

_____ is really sentimental. Back in
(Name)
college, on Valentine's Day _____ would
(he/she)
send _____ mother a heart-shaped box of
(his/her)
laundry.

❏

_____ is so cheap that at _____ own
(Name)   (his/her)
wedding reception, _____ requested
(he/she)
separate checks.

❏

_____ thinks nothing is too good for
(Name)
_____ _____ . And that's what
(his/her) (wife/husband)
_____ gives _____ —nothing.
(Name)   (her/him)

❏

When a local nursing home asked _____
(Name)
for a donation, _____ gave them _____
(he/she)   (his/her)
parents.

❏

_____'s _____ recently had plastic
(Name)   (wife/husband)
surgery—_____ cut _____ Visa card
(Name)   (her/his)
into little pieces.

❏

_____ had a brass band at his wedding.
(Name)
He put it on his wife's finger.

❏

_____'s _____ wanted a con-
(Name)   (wife/husband)
vertible, so _____ bought _____ a
(Name)   (her/him)
rickshaw.

❏

_____ is so cheap that when _____
(Name)   (his/her)
_____ said _____ wanted to see
(wife/husband)   (she/he)
the world, _____ gave _____ a map.
(he/she)   (her/him)

CHEAP

❑

Is_____ cheap? When _____ heard
(Name)   (he/she)
that you can feed a whole family in India for
twenty dollars a year, _____ sent _____
                   (he/she)   (his/her)
family there.

❑

_____ is so cheap that_____ moved
(Name)   (he/she)
into a house next to a nuclear plant, so
_____ could read by the glow of_____
(he/she)   (his/her)
family.

❑

_____ says _____ _____ is
(Name)   (his/her)   (wife/husband)
always asking for money. A couple of weeks
ago_____asked for $200. Last week
    (she/he)
_____asked for $150. This week
(she/he)
_____asked for $100. I asked what
(she/he)
_____ does with it all. _____said, "I
(she/he)   (Name)
don't know—I never give _____ any."
                    (her/him)

❑

One day I went to _____'s office to ask
                 (Name)
for a contribution for the homeless. _____
                                (He/She)
said, "Do you see that old lady in the next
room scrubbing the floor? Well, she needs
an operation but has no money. Now, why
would I give money to the homeless if I won't
help my own mother?"

❑

_____was angry when his wife got her
(Name)
hair professionally colored. "That's too
expensive—when are you going to let your
hair go gray like Barbara Bush?" he
complained. His wife replied, "The day
you're elected president."

CHEAP

❑

_____ is so cheap that instead of paying
(Name)
a doctor for an exam, _____ lies on the
(he/she)
luggage X ray at the airport.

❑

_____ has monogrammed silverware at
(Name)
_____ house. It reads TWA.
(his/her)

❑

One day _____ came across a poor old
(Name)
bum whose worn-out shoe sole was flapping
against the street when he walked. _____
(Name)
took pity and pulled out a big wad of twenty-
dollar bills. Then _____ took the rubber
(he/she)
band off the bankroll and gave it to the bum
to keep his shoe sole from flapping.

HEAVY DRINKER

❑

To call _____ a boozer might be an
(Name)
overstatement. But I've heard that _____
(his/her)
first words as a baby were, "Let's party!"

❑

_____ has had so many battles with the
(Name)
bottle that _____ received the Purple
(he/she)
Heart from Manischevitz.

❑

_____ is writing a song titled, "The
(Name)
Things We Did Last Summer, I'm Taking
Shots for All Winter Long."

❑

_____ drinks so much that _____ is the
(Name)   (he/she)
number-one draft choice of the Betty Ford
Clinic.

HEAVY DRINKER

❑

_____ once went on a liquid diet. In
  (Name)
three weeks, _____ lost twenty-one days.
        (he/she)

❑

_____ isn't always as happy as _____
  (Name)   (he/she)
looks right now. Last week _____ was
                (he/she)
kicked out of a bar so they could start the

happy hour.

❑

I've been trying to figure out what to get

_____ for _____ birthday. I mean,
 (Name)   (his/her)
how do you gift wrap a saloon?

❑

When _____ was in college, _____
   (Name)   (he/she)
majored in parties and graduated *magnum*

cum loaded.

❑

_____ loved to party in college. _____
  (Name)   (He/She)
was always the designated drunk.

❑

_____ graduated from college with a 4.0
  (Name)
average. That was _____ blood-alcohol
           (his/her)
level.

❑

Everyone dreams of writing a hit song, and

_____ is no exception. _____ once
 (Name)   (He/She)
tried to write a drinking song but couldn't get

past the first two bars.

❑

_____ drinks so much that _____
  (Name)   (his/her)
doctor recently found an olive in _____
                    (his/her)
urine specimen.

HEAVY DRINKER

❑

_____ went for a blood test last week
(Name)
and got the results on a little card that read:
"100 proof."

❑

_____ really knows how to hold _____
(Name)   (his/her)
liquor—it's always in a flask in _____ coat
(his/her)
pocket.

❑

_____ had a little accident last week
(Name)
slipping on the ice—it had fallen out of

_____ cocktail glass.
(his/her)

❑

_____ says you've had too many martinis
(Name)
when you *feel* sophisticated, but you can't

say it.

❑

_____ offered _____ bartender some
(Name)   (his/her)
helpful advice the other day. _____ said,
(He/She)
"You know how you can sell more beer? Try

filling the glasses up."

❑

_____ invented a drink combining prune
(Name)
juice and 7-Up. It's called a *Hurry Up.*

❑

Last week I went to meet _____ in our
(Name)
favorite bar. I asked the bartender, "Where's

_____? I'm supposed to meet _____
(Name)   (him/her)
here." The bartender replied, "You're

standing on _____."
(him/her)

❑

_____ once volunteered to write a slogan
(Name)
for *Mothers Against Drunk Driving.* Here's

what _____ came up with: "Don't drink
(he/she)
and drive. It's hard to steer and throw up at

the same time."

HEAVY DRINKER

❑

_____ has no respect for age—unless it's
(Name)
bottled.

❑

_____ recently cut down on his drinking.
(Name)
He says he did it for his "wife and kidneys."

❑

_____ says _____ doesn't drink any-
(Name)   (he/she)
more. Of course, _____ doesn't drink any
                   (he/she)
less either.

❑

A while ago, I was in _____'s neighbor-
                        (Name)
hood and decided to pay a visit. I walked up

to _____ house and called in through the
    (his/her)
screen door, "Is this where_____ lives?"
                              (Name)
_____ _____ called back, "Yes it
(His/Her)   (wife/husband)
is—just carry _____ in, and lay _____
               (him/her)   (him/her)
on the couch."

❑

_____ recently had a serious operation.
(Name)
They removed a bar rail from_____ foot.
                              (his/her)

❑

When _____ drove across the border to
       (Name)
Canada, _____ saw a sign that read:
          (he/she)
"Drink Canada Dry."_____ tried but
                      (Name)
didn't quite succeed.

❑

_____ just invented a new drink made
(Name)
from vodka and Folgers coffee. It's called a
Screw Mrs. Olson.

IMMATURE

☐

You can tell when _____ likes you—
(Name)

_____ lets you hold _____ teddy bear.
(he/she)   (his/her)

☐

I saw an old photo of _____ sitting on
(Name)

Santa's lap in a department store, looking

very happy. It was taken the same year

_____ graduated from high school.
(he/she)

☐

I remember when _____ finally found out
(Name)

the truth about Santa Claus—_____ was
(he/she)

so upset _____ flunked _____ driving
(he/she)   (his/her)

test.

☐

When _____ was younger, _____ once
(Name)   (he/she)

said to _____ dad, "Pop, I have the big-
(his/her)

gest feet in the third grade. Is that because

I'm _____ ?" "No," _____ dad re-
(Nationality)   (his/her)

plied. "It's because you're *nineteen*."

IMMORAL

☐

_____ is a _____ of many con-
(Name)   (man/woman)

victions. In fact, _____ police record is a
(his/her)

mile long.

☐

If Moses had known _____ , there would
(Name)

have been a lot more commandments.

☐

One thing about _____ — _____ is
(Name)   (he/she)

consistent. _____ is taking advantage of
(He/She)

the same people _____ took advantage of
(he/she)

ten years ago.

☐

_____ gets _____ integrity from
(Name)   (his/her)

_____ father, who drives the getaway car
(his/her)

for the "Mob" in Chicago.

IMMORAL

❑

_____ is a fine salesperson. _____
(Name)   (His/Her)
sales technique is just one step ahead of

Breaking and Entering.

❑

_____ is so dishonest, _____ can't
(Name)   (he/she)
even tell the truth without lying.

❑

If you've ever worked with _____, you
                                        (Name)
know that _____ does the work of two
                  (he/she)
people—Frank and Jesse James.

❑

It's good to see you out there in front of me,

_____. It means you're not stabbing me
(Name)
in the back.

❑

_____ would never give you a bum steer.
(Name)
_____ would rather sell it to you.
(He/She)

❑

_____ says that _____ always has a
(Name)   (he/she)
clear conscience. But actually, I think it's just

a case of bad memory.

❑

I had a strange dream the other night that I

died and went to the gates of heaven. But I

was told that in order to get into heaven, I'd

have to write my sins on the steps leading to

the Pearly Gates. So, I started writing in

chalk—one sin for each step—when, who

should I see but _____. _____ was
                              (Name)   (He/She)
coming down for more chalk.

SMOKER

❑

_____ hasn't bought a cigarette in years.
(Name)

_____ brother is a janitor.
(His/Her)

❑

It took a lot of willpower, but finally _____
(Name)
gave up trying to quit smoking.

❑

I was at _____'s office the other day and
(Name)
went into the men's room. There was a sign
that read: "Don't put cigarettes in the urinals
—it makes them soggy and hard to light."

❑

_____ was standing in a no-smoking
(Name)
area when a cop pointed to a cigarette on
the floor. The cop demanded, "Is that
yours?" "Naw," said _____. "Go ahead
(Name)
and take it—you saw it first."

❑

_____ smokes a brand of cigarettes that
(Name)
gives coupons. _____ has so many
(He/She)
coupons now that _____ can get a free
(he/she)
tombstone.

❑

With the high price of cigarettes, _____
(Name)
recently switched brands. _____ used to
(He/She)
smoke Luckies and Camels. Lately, _____
(he/she)
smokes OP's—other people's.

❑

Everyone is conscious of the dangers of
smoking these days. _____ tried very
(Name)
hard to quit and finally joined *Cigarettes
Anonymous*. The way it works is if you have
a terrific urge to smoke, you call up another
member of *Cigarettes Anonymous* and go
out together and get drunk.

Family Life

CHILDHOOD

❏

_____was so unwanted that when
(Name)

_____was born, _____ father gave out
(he/she)   (his/her)

cigar butts.

❏

_____never felt wanted. For example,
(Name)

one night _____'s house caught on fire,
(Name)

and _____ parents yelled, "_____, go
(his/her)   (Name)

to your room!"

❏

The problem with _____ is that when
(Name)

_____ mother used to rock _____ to
(his/her)   (him/her)

sleep, she didn't use big enough rocks.

❏

_____'s parents gave _____ unusual
(Name)   (him/her)

bathtub toys—a hair dryer and a radio—

plugged in.

❏

_____ had a rough childhood. For the
(Name)

first seven years of _____ life, _____
(his/her)   (he/she)

answered to the name, "Hey You."

❏

_____ was so unwanted as a child that
(Name)

_____ parents used to urge _____ to
(his/her)   (him/her)

run outside and play in the freeway.

❏

As a child, _____ always complained to
(Name)

_____ parents that _____ didn't feel
(his/her)   (he/she)

wanted. So they put _____ picture up in
(his/her)

the post office.

❏

_____ learned to swim at a very early
(Name)

age. _____ father would row _____ out
(His/Her)   (him/her)

to the middle of the lake, throw _____
(him/her)

overboard, and make _____ swim back.
(him/her)

The toughest part was getting out of that sack.

CHILDHOOD

❑

_____ was kidnapped once. But _____
(Name)   (his/her)
parents refused to pay the ransom—they

didn't want to break a ten.

❑

_____ was so unloved as a child that
(Name)
one Halloween _____ parents dressed
                        (his/her)
_____ up as a speed bump.
(him/her)

❑

_____ never felt wanted as a child.
(Name)
_____ mother used to wrap _____
(His/Her)   (his/her)
school lunch in a road map.

❑

When _____ was a child _____ hated
        (Name)   (he/she)
playing Hide and Seek. Nobody ever

wanted to find _____ .
                    (him/her)

❑

When _____ was little, _____ grand-
        (Name)   (his/her)
pa came to visit, and _____ asked him if
                            (he/she)
he still played football. Grandpa asked little

_____ what made _____ think he was
(Name)   (him/her)
a football player. _____ answered, "Well,
                        (Name)
my dad says we're going to get a lot of

money when you kick off."

❑

When _____ was sixteen, _____ dad
        (Name)   (his/her)
warned _____ never to go to an X-rated
            (him/her)
theater because _____ might see some-
                        (he/she)
thing _____ shouldn't see. But, one
        (he/she)
Saturday, _____ yielded to temptation
                (Name)
and went to one. Sure enough, _____
                                        (he/she)
saw something _____ shouldn't see—
                    (he/she)
_____ dad.
(his/her)

HOMETOWN

☐

_____ hails from _____. Last sum-
(Name)   (City/State)
mer, a tornado hit and did $10 million worth

of improvements.

☐

In _____'s hometown, the welcome to
(Name)
town and leaving town signs are on the

same post.

☐

_____'s hometown is so boring, they
(Name)
used to go to Kmart just to try on gloves.

☐

_____ comes from a really small town.
(Name)
It's so small that the McDonald's has only

one arch—and you have to order a Big Mac

out of a catalog. The town is so small, they

had to close the zoo when the butterfly died.

MARRIAGE

☐

_____ and _____ _____ tied the
(Name)   (his/her)   (wife/husband)
knot in one of those little chapels in Las

Vegas—it was called "Our Lady of the

Strip."

☐

_____ and _____ _____ started
(Name)   (his/her)   (wife/husband)
off their marriage as a very happy couple. It

wasn't until they left the church that it began

to fizzle.

☐

_____, you've given your _____
(Name)   (wife/husband)
something to live for—a divorce.

☐

The family doctor called _____'s
(Name)
_____ the other day and said, "I
(wife/husband)
don't like the way your _____ looks."
(husband/wife)
_____'s _____ said, "Neither do
(Name)   (wife/husband)
I, but _____ is good to the kids."
(he/she)

MARRIAGE

☐

_____ and _____ _____ had their
(Name)   (his/her) (wife/husband)
picture taken last week. The photographer
told them to look natural, so they started
bickering.

☐

_____'s _____ does bird imita-
(Name)   (wife/husband)
tions— _____ watches _____ like a
          (she/he)   (him/her)
hawk.

☐

At _____'s house, every other Friday is
     (Name)
Academy Awards night—_____ brings
                              (Name)
home _____ paycheck, and _____
      (his/her)   (his/her)
_____ says, "The envelope, please."
(wife/husband)

☐

The first time _____ met _____
                 (Name)   (his/her)
_____ was at a singles bar—_____
(wife/husband)   (he/she)
invited _____ up to _____ apartment
         (her/him)   (his/her)
for a scotch and sofa.

NEIGHBORHOOD

☐

_____ came from such a tough neigh-
(Name)
borhood that anyone with more than one
eye had to be from somewhere else.

☐

In _____'s neighborhood, if you weren't
    (Name)
home by 10:00 P.M. you could be declared
legally dead.

☐

_____'s neighborhood was so tough that
(Name)
every kid in _____ elementary school had
              (his/her)
to write an essay titled: "*If* I grow up."

☐

The neighborhood high school _____
                               (Name)
attended was so tough, it had its own
coroner and the school colors were black
and blue.

Lifestyle

POOR

☐

_____'s family was so poor they had to
(Name)
go to Kentucky Fried Chicken and lick other
people's fingers.

☐

_____'s family couldn't afford a sand-
(Name)
box, so_____ had to play in the cat's litter
(he/she)
box. The trouble was, the cat kept trying to
cover _____ up.
(him/her)

☐

_____'s family used to gather around the
(Name)
mailbox each day, in the hope of getting a
care package from Ethiopia.

☐

When_____was a child, _____ family
(Name)   (his/her)
was so poor that their Christmas tree would
not have had any decorations at all if their
grandpa hadn't sneezed.

RICH

☐

_____'s family was so rich _____
(Name)   (he/she)
wore Gucci diapers.

☐

_____'s family once promised _____
(Name)   (him/her)
a trip to Disneyland just for not wetting the
bed.

☐

_____'s family was so rich that instead
(Name)
of dimes, the Tooth Fairy brought stocks and
bonds.

☐

_____almost had a nervous breakdown
(Name)
at age seven when_____ mother ran out
(his/her)
of Grey Poupon.

RICH

☐

_____ came from a very wealthy family.
(Name)
_____ father used to do the spring plow-
(His/Her)
ing with a Rolls Royce.

☐

_____ has done well in life. Every year
(Name)
_____ sends _____ Easter eggs to Ted
(he/she)   (his/her)
Turner to be colorized.

☐

_____ is so wealthy that _____ wrote a
(Name)   (he/she)
check the other day, and the bank bounced.

☐

_____ had a bad accident the other
(Name)
day— _____ dropped _____ billfold,
       (he/she)   (his/her)
and it broke _____ toe.
              (his/her)

SPORTS AND HOBBIES

☐

_____ was very athletic in high school.
(Name)
He always won top honors in the "breast
stroke."

☐

_____ was very excited about a new
(Name)
hobby, until _____ _____
              (his/her) (wife/husband)
found about _____ .
             (her/him)

☐

You may not know that _____ was in the
                       (Name)
Olympics. _____ was the javelin catcher.
           (He/She)

☐

_____ is no card shark. _____ can't
(Name)   (He/She)
win at poker even when _____ cheats.
                        (he/she)

SPORTS AND HOBBIES

❑

_____ stopped playing on the high
(Name)
school hockey team in his senior year—they

finally got a real hockey puck

❑

I don't want to accuse _____ of cheating
(Name)
at golf, but _____ once shot a hole in one
(he/she)
and wrote a zero in _____ scorecard.
(his/her)

❑

Some of you may know that _____ is an
(Name)
avid weekend golfer. Apparently, _____
(he/she)
doesn't have enough frustration during the

week.

❑

_____ has a neat gadget that helps
(Name)
_____ take five strokes off _____ golf
(him/her)   (his/her)
score. It's called an eraser.

❑

_____'s _____ claims it's a sin to
(Name)   (wife/husband)
play golf on Sunday. _____ right—the
(She's/He's)
way _____ plays golf, it *is* a sin.
(Name)

❑

_____ always wins at cards but rarely at
(Name)
the track. _____ can't get a horse up
(He/She)
_____ sleeve.
(his/her)

❑

_____ was quite a football player in his
(Name)
younger days. His specialty was to butt his

head against the opponents' helmet. It

earned him a nickname that follows him to

this day—"Butt Head."

❑

_____ has a very unique hobby.
(Name)
_____ lies under _____ bed and
(He/She)   (his/her)
collects dust.

SPORTS AND HOBBIES

❑

The other day, _____ was at the race
(Name)
track and bet on a horse that was so slow, it
was arrested for loitering.

❑

_____ and _____ buddies went on a
(Name)   (his/her)
fishing trip, and one of the guys didn't get a
bite all day—so _____ bit him.
(Name)

❑

_____ doesn't have the straightest shot—
(Name)
particularly when he takes a few nips from
the flask in his hunting jacket. Once he
aimed at a duck but hit a frog. He picked it
up, scratched his head, and said, "Looks like
I knocked its feathers off."

TRAVEL

❑

_____ told me that _____ flight to
(Name)   (his/her)
Europe was so rough the flight attendant
poured the food right into the airsickness
bags.

❑

When _____ returned from _____
(Name)   (his/her)
vacation, _____ quipped, "Travel is
(he/she)
broadening, but so is strawberry shortcake."

❑

_____ has been traveling a lot recently.
(Name)
Last month _____ visited a city where the
(he/she)
taxi drivers don't speak English—New York.

❑

_____ recently decided to go on a long
(Name)
vacation to forget everything. When _____
(he/she)
got to _____ hotel in Hawaii, _____
(his/her)   (he/she)
opened _____ suitcase and discovered
(his/her)
_____ had forgotten everything.
(he/she)

TRAVEL

❑

_____ is the only person I know who
(Name)
went to Mexico and came back constipated.

❑

_____ is quite a seasoned traveler. Last
(Name)
month _____ traveled to Los Angeles and
(he/she)
had to rest for two days to recover from bus

lag.

❑

_____ recently stayed in a hotel in San
(Name)
Francisco. Guess what _____ found in one
(he/she)
of the drawers? Tony Bennett's heart.

❑

Every winter, _____ flies down to Puerto
(Name)
Rico to visit _____ hubcaps.
(his/her)

UNSUCCESSFUL

❑

Waiting for _____ to make it big is like
(Name)
leaving a light on for Jimmy Hoffa.

❑

_____'s retail business is so slow that
(Name)
even the shoplifters have stopped coming.

❑

The things that _____ has accomplished
(Name)
in life can be counted on _____ little
(his/her)
finger.

❑

When _____ came to town, _____ had
(Name)   (he/she)
a beat-up fifteen-year-old car and $400 in

cash. Today, _____ has two brand-new
(he/she)
Cadillacs and a $300,000 mortgage. Now

that's progress!

UNSUCCESSFUL

❑

_____ has many friends in high places.
(Name)
Trouble is, they all throw coconuts.

❑

_____ was once a key _____ in the
(Name)   (man/woman)
gasoline business—when someone had to

use the restroom, _____ would hand out
                        (he/she)
the key.

❑

_____ recently got a job as a sales-
(Name)
person. The first day, _____ got two
                              (he/she)
orders: "Get out and stay out."

❑

You might find this hard to believe, but

_____'s hometown is making a statue of
(Name)

_____ . But they're delayed right now
(him/her)
because they ran out of Silly Putty.

Personality

BORING

❏

_____ is a person of few words—which
 (Name)

_____ repeats over and over and over.
 (he/she)

❏

Talking to _____ reminds people of an oil
 (Name)

driller—if _____ doesn't strike oil in forty
 (he/she)

minutes, _____ keeps on boring.
 (he/she)

❏

_____'s idea of a hot evening is turning
 (Name)

up the thermostat.

❏

_____'s life is so boring _____ can
 (Name)   (he/she)

only look forward to a "Maalox moment."

❏

_____ sure lives life on the edge. _____
 (Name)   (His/Her)

idea of living dangerously is eating cottage

cheese on the expiration date.

❏

When I look into _____'s glassy eyes, I
                   (Name)

sometimes wonder if _____ is alive or just
                       (he/she)

well-embalmed.

❏

_____ leads such a dull life that _____
 (Name)   (he/she)

can actually write _____ diary one week
                     (his/her)

in advance.

❏

_____ went to a shrink and said, "Doc,
 (Name)

you've got to help me. I'm always talking to

myself." The shrink said, "Don't worry about

that—a lot of people do." And _____
                                 (Name)

said, "Yeah, I know. But Doc, I'm so *boring.*"

CRAZY

☐

_____ once said, and I quote, "Of all the
(Name)
things I've lost, I miss my mind the most."

☐

One of_____'s greatest accomplish-
(Name)
ments was graduating with honors from

Psychotic State University.

☐

_____ is so paranoid that at football
(Name)
games, when the players go into a huddle,

_____ thinks they're talking about
(he/she)

_____ .
(him/her)

☐

_____ was once under the delusion that
(Name)
_____ was a horse. _____ even started
(he/she)   (He/She)
eating oats and whinnying a lot. I think the

payoff was that before a psychiatrist finally

cured_____,_____ won the Kentucky Derby.
(him/her) (he/she)

DISHONEST

☐

_____ 's philosophy is: "Be sincere—
(Name)
whether you mean it or not."

☐

_____ is always bragging that _____
(Name)   (he/she)
went to Penn State. I did a little checking and

found out that it was actually *state pen.*

☐

If you watch carefully, you can tell when

_____ is lying—_____ lips are moving.
(Name)   (his/her)

☐

_____ suffered a serious accident on a
(Name)
recent fishing trip. _____ dislocated
(He/She)
_____ shoulders while describing the fish
(his/her)
that got away.

EGOTISTICAL

❏

Tonight we gather to honor a living legend—

_____ is a legend in _____ own mind.
(Name)   (his/her)

❏

When _____ was born, _____ weighed
(Name)   (he/she)

thirteen pounds. Of course, most of that was

ego.

❏

_____ thinks _____ is quite a big
(Name)   (he/she)

wheel. Of course, you know what dogs do

on wheels.

❏

I don't want to say that _____ is ego-
(Name)

tistical, but when _____ graduated from
(he/she)

high school, _____ wanted to join the
(he/she)

Navy so the world could see _____ .
(him/her)

❏

If _____ had _____ life to live over,
(Name)   (his/her)

_____ would still fall in love with
(he/she)

_____ .
(himself/herself)

❏

_____ doesn't expect special treatment.
(Name)

_____ just wants to be treated like any
(He/She)

other *great person.*

❏

Is _____ egotistical? Well, when some-
(Name)

body sneezes, _____ says, "I bless you."
(he/she)

And, once a day _____ calls dial-a-prayer
(he/she)

to see if _____ has any messages.
(he/she)

❏

Every year on _____ birthday, _____
(his/her)   (Name)

sends a congratulations card to _____
(his/her)

parents.

45

EGOTISTICAL

❏

_____ plans to give a talk on humility—
(Name)

just as soon as _____ can find a large
(he/she)

enough hall.

❏

_____ 's employees can't help admiring
(Name)

_____ . If they don't, _____ fires them.
(him/her)   (he/she)

❏

_____ is so egotistical that in _____
(Name)   (his/her)

will, _____ leaves everything to
(he/she)

_____ .
(himself/herself)

❏

_____ was selected to be _____ .
(Name)   (Position/Honor)

But _____ co-workers said "Frankly, we
(his/her)

would be happier if _____ was named
(he/she)

Pope because then all we'd have to do is

kiss _____ ring."
(his/her)

LAZY

❏

_____ is so lazy, they named a shoe after
(Name)

_____ —the loafer.
(him/her)

❏

Even _____ 's car is shiftless.
(Name)

❏

_____ always gives _____
(Name)   (Company/Organization)

an honest day's work. Of course, it usually

takes _____ a week to do it.
(him/her)

❏

_____ has been called a "miracle
(Name)

worker." When _____ works, it's a
(he/she)

miracle.

LOSER

❑

_____ has a lot of degrees: a B.A., an
(Name)
M.A., a Ph.D.—but no J.O.B.

❑

After a lot of searching, _____ has finally
(Name)
found a job that will pay what _____ is
(he/she)
worth—but the salary doesn't cover

_____ busfare.
(his/her)

❑

Someday _____ will find _____ ,
(Name)   (himself/herself)
and boy will _____ be disillusioned.
(he/she)

❑

I'm very happy for _____. _____ is finally
(Name)   (He/She)
starting to move up in the world— _____
(he/she)
has a job as an elevator operator.

❑

_____ is such a loser, _____ gives
(Name)   (he/she)
failure a bad name.

❑

_____ lacks only two things for reaching
(Name)
the top: talent and ambition.

❑

_____ is as broke as a pickpocket in a
(Name)
nudist camp.

❑

_____ left _____ job due to illness and
(Name)   (his/her)
fatigue. _____ boss got sick and tired of
(His/Her)

_____ .
(him/her)

NASTY

❑

_____ was a really bratty kid. _____
(Name)   (He/She)
used to put Super Glue in _____ dad's
(his/her)
Preparation H and hide _____ grandpa's
(his/her)
bedpan in the freezer.

❑

When _____ was young, someone gave
(Name)
_____ this bad advice: "Be yourself."
(him/her)

❑

_____ was the only kid I knew who was
(Name)
abandoned by an orphanage.

❑

_____ is the kind of person who would
(Name)
go to Stevie Wonder's house and rearrange
the furniture.

❑

You might not know that our good friend

_____ was a four-letter man in school.
(Name)
Of course, I can't repeat those four letters.

❑

Last week, _____ made a killing in the
(Name)
stock market. _____ shot _____ broker.
(He/She)   (his/her)

❑

You think Rambo is nasty? Last month

_____ gave the Los Angeles Police
(Name)
Department lessons on how to fight dirty.

❑

Of all the people I know, _____ has the
(Name)
most chutzpah. _____ once borrowed a
(He/She)
friend's Mercedes, and then called him later
to say, "I have good news for you—your air
bag works."

NASTY

❑

_____ doesn't have ulcers—_____
(Name)   (he/she)
gives them.

❑

_____ has the disposition of an untipped
(Name)
waiter.

❑

_____ is known as "the great do-it-
(Name)
yourselfer"—whenever anyone asks_____
(him/her)
to do something, _____ says, "Do it
(he/she)
yourself."

❑

When driving a car_____ often uses a
(Name)
finger signal which really means: "Do unto
yourself what you're apparently trying to do
unto me."

STUPID

❑

_____ is so stupid_____can't even
(Name)   (he/she)
spell I.R.S.

❑

Want to know how to put a gleam in

_____ 's eyes? Just shine a flashlight in
(Name)
one of_____ears.
(his/her)

❑

_____ keeps complaining of headaches.
(Name)
_____ , if I've told you once, I've told you
(Name)
a hundred times—when you get out of bed,
it's *feet* first.

❑

_____ once hijacked a submarine.
(Name)
_____ demanded $100,000 and a
(He/She)
parachute.

STUPID

❏

_____ once bought a birthday cake for
(Name)
_____ brother and wanted to write
(his/her)
Happy Birthday on it. But _____ couldn't
(he/she)
get the cake into the typewriter.

❏

I asked _____ , "If you found a million
(Name)
dollars, would you try to find the owner and
return it?" _____ answered, "Only if it
(Name)
belonged to a *poor* person."

❏

Last week _____ stayed up all night
(Name)
studying for _____ urine test.
(his/her)

❏

_____ 's tailor quoted _____ $600 for
(Name)   (him/her)
a suit made from virgin wool. _____ asked,
(Name)
"How much would you charge for a suit
made from a sheep that fooled around a
little?"

❏

_____ doesn't read a lot, but _____
(Name)   (he/she)
does have two books in _____ library—
(his/her)
one of them hasn't even been colored in yet.

❏

When _____ was driving to Cleveland to
(Name)
visit _____ cousin, _____ saw a sign
(his/her)   (he/she)
that read: "Cleveland Left." So, _____
(he/she)
turned around and drove back home.

❏

_____ is so stupid, _____ thinks
(Name)   (he/she)
J. Edgar Hoover was a vacuum cleaner.

❏

_____ was once hired by N.A.S.A. to go
(Name)
up in a rocket with a monkey. The monkey's
job was to work the dials and instruments,
and _____ 's job was to feed the monkey.
(Name)

STUPID

❑

_____ is a little slow. It takes _____ an
(Name)   (him/her)
hour and a half to watch "60 Minutes."

❑

I recently took _____ out to a French
(Name)
restaurant, and _____ ordered the soup
(he/she)
du jour of the day.

❑

_____ tried to snort coke once, but
(Name)
_____ couldn't get the bottle in _____
(he/she)   (his/her)
nose.

❑

_____ is so stupid, _____ thinks that
(Name)   (he/she)
Taco Bell is a Mexican telephone company.

❑

Somebody once called _____ "illiterate."
(Name)
_____ got very indignant and said, "I'll
(He/She)
have you know my parents were married

when I was born."

❑

I've heard that _____ has a photographic
(Name)
mind. Too bad it never developed.

❑

Last week the I.R.S. called _____ for a tax
(Name)
audit. They told _____ they wanted to see
(him/her)
_____ records, so _____ brought in
(his/her)   (he/she)
seven Lawrence Welks and ten Barbra

Streisands.

❑

_____ drove around the block twenty
(Name)
times yesterday afternoon— _____
(his/her)
direction signal was stuck.

STUPID

☐

_____ is the kind of person who gets in a
(Name)
revolving door and stops to tie_____shoe.
(his/her)

☐

I asked _____ if_____ had trouble
(Name)   (he/she)
making up _____ mind. _____ an-
(his/her)   (He/She)
swered, "Yes and no."

☐

Don't get me wrong—_____'s mind
(Name)
actually contains a wealth of knowledge—

_____ just can't remember any of it.
(he/she)

☐

_____ reminds me of a bottle of beer.
(Name)
Both are empty from the neck up.

☐

You've heard about people who follow a

different drummer. Well, _____ follows a
(Name)
different organ grinder.

☐

Back in _____ high school days,_____
(his/her)   (Name)
was in a spelling bee. They asked _____
(him/her)
to spell Mississippi. _____ answered,
(Name)
"Which one, the river or the state?"

☐

_____ is a literary person. All the words
(Name)
on _____ tatoo are spelled right.
(his/her)

☐

_____ recently went to a department
(Name)
store to buy a brassiere for his wife. He

asked the clerk for a size seven-and-a-half.

"How did you get *that* measurement?" the

clerk asked. _____ said, "With my hat."
(Name)

52

TASTELESS

❑

_____'s idea of a gourmet meal is
(Name)
Twinkies and Cheez Whiz.

❑

_____, I saw you driving your car the
(Name)
other day. Tell me, was anyone *hurt* in that

wreck?

❑

_____ recently drove_____ car into a
(Name)   (his/her)
used-car lot to see what they would give

_____ for it. They offered _____ ten
(him/her)   (him/her)
dollars to drive it off the lot.

❑

_____ drove up to a highway tollbooth
(Name)
the other day, and the attendant said, "Fifty

cents."_____ replied, "Sold."
(Name)

❑

_____, I love the decor in your house. It
(Name)
looks like early Salvation Army.

❑

I asked_____ what _____ thought
(Name)   (he/she)
about Red China. _____ said if you have
(He/She)
a yellow tablecloth, it should be fairly

attractive.

❑

_____ is very proud of_____ art
(Name)   (his/her)
collection. _____ recently invited me over
(He/She)
to view _____ latest acquisitions: a picture
(his/her)
of Elvis painted on black velvet and a lava

lamp.

❑

_____ has a razor-sharp wit. Last summer
(Name)
_____ was in the hospital, and every time
(he/she)
someone knocked on _____ door, _____
(his/her)   (he/she)
would call out, "Who goes there? Friend or

enema?"

UNLUCKY

❑

_____ doesn't have much luck—yester-
(Name)
day_____artificial flower died.
(his/her)

❑

The last time _____ stopped and smelled
(Name)
the roses, a bee stung _____ on the nose.
(him/her)

❑

Last week _____ dined in a restaurant
(Name)
where the catch of the day was hepatitis.

❑

_____ recently went to Las Vegas in a
(Name)
$30,000 Cadillac and came back in a

$400,000 Greyhound bus.

❑

_____ is in big trouble. First _____
(Name)   (his/her)
drycleaner called and said they'd lost

_____ shirt. Then _____ stockbroker
(his/her)   (his/her)
called and said the same thing.

❑

_____ finally won a custody battle with
(Name)
_____ "ex" in divorce court. _____ got
(his/her)   (He/She)
custody of_____ in-laws.
(his/her)

❑

Last week, _____ bet on a horse that was
(Name)
so slow the jockey kept a diary.

❑

_____ recently did some research on
(Name)
_____ family tree. _____ found out
(his/her)   (He/She)
_____ was the sap.
(he/she)

UNLUCKY   UNPOPULAR

❑

When _____ took golf lessons last
     (Name)
summer, the golf pro kept telling___ ___ to
                                (him/her)
keep_____ head down. So _____
    (his/her)   (Name)
did—and somebody stole _____ golf cart.
                        (his/her)

❑

_____ is so unlucky that when _____
  (Name)   (he/she)
told the suicide hot line counselor that_____
                                       (he/she)
was going to kill _____ , she replied,
               (himself/herself)
"You're doing the right thing."

❑

Bad luck seems to run in _____'s family.
                          (Name)
Did you know that_____ father used to be
               (his/her)
a prize fighter? That's right, he fought 100
times. I asked him, "How many fights did
you win?" He answered, "None." I said,
"You lost 100 fights?" He replied, "You can't
win 'em all."

❑

_____ was so unpopular as a kid, even
 (Name)
_____ imaginary playmate wouldn't play
(his/her)
with _____ .
    (him/her)

❑

_____ was such an unpopular kid that
 (Name)
_____ parents had to tie a pork chop
(his/her)
around _____ neck to get the dog to play
      (his/her)
with _____ .
    (him/her)

❑

_____ had only one date in high school.
 (Name)
They got along pretty well until _____
                               (his/her)
date's seeing-eye dog bit _____on the
                          (Name)
leg.

❑

_____ is so unpopular that even _____
 (Name)   (his/her)
inflatable _____ has a migraine.
          (girlfriend/boyfriend)

UNPOPULAR

❑

_____ once sent _____ photograph to
(Name)   (his/her)

the Lonely Hearts Club. _____ got back
                                      (He/She)

the reply: "We're not *that* lonely."

❑

Do you know what _____ found out after
                              (Name)

spending $5,000 on plastic surgery? No

one liked _____ anyway.
                 (him/her)

❑

Asking people what they think of _____ is
                                           (Name)

like asking a fire hydrant what it thinks of

dogs.

❑

_____ was so unpopular as a kid that
(Name)

_____ had to be _____ own best friend.
(he/she)   (his/her)

❑

_____ loves to sing. He's usually asked to
(Name)

sing tenor—ten or fifteen miles away.

❑

_____ was once set up on a blind date
(Name)

with a _____ named _____ .
          (woman/man)   (Jane/John)

When the two first met, _____ asked, "Are
                                   (Name)

you _____ ?" And _____ replied,
       (Jane/John)   (Jane/John)

"Are you _____ ?" _____ said, "Yes," to
            (Name)   (Name)

which _____ responded, "Then, I'm not
          (Jane/John)

_____ ."
(Jane/John)

❑

When _____ was in high school, _____
          (Name)   (he/she)

was voted "Most likely to go to seed."

WEIRD

❑

_____ had an uncle who proclaimed he
(Name)
was psychic. He knew the exact day he was
going to die—the warden told him.

❑

_____ once bought a dog with no legs. I
(Name)
asked _____ what _____ named it,
(him/her)   (he/she)
and _____ said, "He doesn't have a name.
(he/she)
If I called him, he couldn't come anyway."

❑

It's not surprising that _____ is extremely
(Name)
shy since _____ comes from such a shy
(he/she)
family. In fact, _____ ancestors came over
(his/her)
on the *Wallflower*.

❑

_____ is working on a new invention. It's
(Name)
a brand of dog food that tastes like a post-
man's ankle.

❑

The other day, _____ told me that
(Name)
_____ thinks _____ is losing _____
(he/she)   (he/she)   (his/her)
memory. I said, "When did you first notice
it?" _____ replied, "Notice *what*?"
(Name)

❑

_____ is so neat that _____ puts news-
(Name)   (he/she)
paper under the cuckoo clock.

❑

_____ has a mind that reminds me of an
(Name)
auction . . . . Going, going, gone.

❑

_____ told me that _____ was a
(Name)   (he/she)
vegetarian, but I once saw _____ eating
(him/her)
meat. _____ explained, "I don't believe in
(Name)
killing animals for food. I only eat animals
who commit suicide."

WIMPY

☐

Whenever someone calls _____ a wimp,
(Name)
_____ says, "Oh yeah? I can tear a
(he/she)
phone book in half!" Then _____ does—
(he/she)
one page at a time.

☐

_____ always gets the last word in a
(Name)
family argument: "Yes, dear."

☐

_____ was boasting to me that his wife
(Name)
comes crawling to him on her hands and
knees. I found out it's because when she gets
mad, _____ hides under the bed.
(Name)

☐

_____ told me that _____ called
(Name)   (he/she)
_____ boss every four-letter word in the
(his/her)
book. I asked, "What did your boss say?"
_____ said, "He didn't say anything—I
(Name)
hung up before he could recognize my voice."

Profession

DOCTOR

❑

_____ recently went to _____ doctor
(Name)   (his/her)
for a checkup. The doctor grabbed _____
(him/her)
by the billfold and said, "Now, cough."

❑

_____ once wanted to become a doctor,
(Name)
but _____ couldn't qualify— _____
(he/she)   (his/her)
handwriting was too legible.

❑

_____ went to the doctor the other day,
(Name)
complaining that one of _____ legs was
(his/her)
hurting. _____ asked, "What should I do,
(He/She)
Doc?" The doctor said, "Limp."

❑

_____ thinks medicine is a great pro-
(Name)
fession—you get a _____ to take off
(woman/man)
_____ clothes, and then you send _____
(her/his)   (her/his)
_____ the bill.
(husband/wife)

❑

After undergoing extensive medical testing,

_____ said, "Doc, tell me honestly, how
(Name)
do I stand?" The doctor replied, "That's what

puzzles me."

❑

_____ earns an excellent living from the
(Name)
practice of medicine. _____ specialty is
(His/Her)
open-wallet surgery.

❑

_____ had a checkup the other day. The
(Name)
nurse told him to strip to the waist, so he took

off his pants.

❑

When _____ was a kid, the _____ next
(Name)   (girl/boy)
door told _____ , "I'll show you mine if
(him/her)
you'll show me yours." So they played

doctor, and _____ had so much fun that
(Name)
_____ decided to make a career of it.
(he/she)

LAWYER

❑

If I were the President, I'd appoint _____
(Name)
to the Supreme Court. After all, we've had a
Frankfurter and a Burger—why not a turkey?

❑

It was so cold around here last winter that
_____ was actually seen with _____
(Name)   (his/her)
hands in _____ own pockets.
         (his/her)

❑

_____ is a hard-working lawyer, as you
(Name)
might know. Last week _____ stayed up all
                      (he/she)
night with a widow, trying to break her will.

❑

_____, a lawyer, is famous for_____
(Name)   (his/her)
advice on how to avoid divorce: "Don't get
married."

❑

_____ is very attached to _____ dog.
(Name)   (his/her)
They first met while chasing the same
ambulance.

❑

I told _____ I needed some legal advice
       (Name)
and asked _____ how much _____
          (him/her)   (he/she)
would charge. _____ replied, "How
              (Name)
much money do you have?"

❑

Do you know the difference between God
and our lawyer friend, _____? God
                       (Name)
doesn't claim to be a lawyer.

❑

_____, do you know what's black and
(Name)
brown and looks good on a lawyer? A
Doberman.

MISCELLANEOUS CAREERS

❏

_____ is to _____ what
(Name)   (occupation/profession)
Roseanne Arnold is to singing.

❏

_____ is no quitter. _____ stays at the
(Name)   (He/She)
same job until _____ gets fired.
              (he/she)

❏

Last week I visited _____ 's office, and
                    (Name)
_____ showed me _____ business
(he/she)   (his/her)
card—it was filled out in pencil.

❏

_____ wanted to study veterinary
(Name)
medicine _and_ taxidermy in college. _____
                                      (He/She)
figured that no matter what happened you'd

always get your dog back.

❏

_____ was once a diamond cutter—
(Name)
_____ trimmed the grass on the baseball
(he/she)
field.

❏

_____ recently joined several other
(Name)
ministers in starting a bowling team. They're

called the "Holy Rollers."

❏

Did you know _____ was once a
             (Name)
bartender? A guy walked into _____ 's
                             (Name)
bar one day and said, "I'd like something

tall, cold, and full of gin." _____ said,
                              (Name)
"Leave my _____ out of this."
          (wife/husband)

❏

As a performer, _____ is most popular
                (Name)
with "mature" audiences. The average age

of _____ last audience was "deceased."
   (his/her)

POLITICIAN

❑

_____ said in one of_____ most stir-
(Name)   (his/her)
ring political speeches, "For years they lied
to you. For years they cheated you. For years
they stole from you. Now give *me* a chance."

❑

To say that_____is conservative is an
(Name)
understatement—_____is slightly to the
(Name)
right of Attila the Hun.

❑

To say that_____is liberal is an under-
(Name)
statement—_____is slightly to the left of
(Name)
Karl Marx.

❑

With a politician like _____, you always
(Name)
know where _____is going and what
(he/she)
_____is doing—_____ is going to the
(he/she)   (he/she)
bank with your money.

SPEAKER

❑

_____'s speeches are about as
(Name)
memorable as Millard Fillmore's vice
president.

❑

_____ has spoken at many meetings and
(Name)
has never been booed. It's hard to boo when
you're yawning.

❑

_____ puts a lot of fire in _____
(Name)   (his/her)
speeches. And a lot of_____ audiences
(his/her)
have wished_____would put more of
(he/she)
_____ speeches in the fire.
(his/her)

❑

_____ has given hundreds of speeches,
(Name)
and _____ audiences never complain—
(his/her)
they just leave.

Religion and Nationality

CATHOLIC

JEWISH

❑

You might not know it, but _____ was
                          (Name)
married in a Catholic church—it was called
"Our Lady of Perpetual Guilt."

❑

_____ , I noticed you don't drink very
(Name)
often. You know why Jews don't drink? It
interferes with their suffering.

❑

When _____ goes to church, the priests
        (Name)
draw lots to see who gets to hear _____
                                  (his/her)
confession.

❑

_____ told me about Jewish foreplay—a
(Name)
half hour of begging.

❑

You've heard of the Ramblin' Wreck from
Georgia Tech? Well, _____ is known as
                     (Name)
the "Total Loss from Holy Cross."

❑

_____ explained to me why Jewish
(Name)
people have large noses—air is free.

❑

_____ talked to a priest who suggested
(Name)
_____ try the rhythm method. "Don't be
(he/she)
silly," said_____ . "Where would I find a
             (Name)
band at 2:00 in the morning?"

❑

_____ can tell you why Jewish divorces
(Name)
cost so much—because they're worth it.

JEWISH

❑

_____ told me why a Jewish wife closes
(Name)
her eyes when making love: She hates to see
her husband having a good time.

❑

_____ is half Jewish and half Italian. If
(Name)
_____ can't get it for you wholesale,
(he/she)
_____ steal it.
(he'll/she'll)

❑

_____ told me she was asked to star in a
(Name)
new Jewish porn movie—_Debbie Does
Nothing._

❑

As you may know, _____ is a very
(Name)
wealthy Jewish _____ who's on ex-
(man/woman)
cellent speaking terms with God. Recently,

_____ decided to make some changes in
(Name)
_____ life. A plastic surgeon gave _____
(his/her)   (him/her)
a new nose, a dentist capped _____ teeth,
(his/her)
and a hairstylist changed _____ graying
(his/her)
hair to its original color. To top it off, _____
(Name)
bought a new Rolls Royce. When _____
(Name)
was driving home in _____ new car,
(his/her)
_____ missed a curve and had a horrible
(he/she)
accident. Lying in the hospital, _____
(he/she)
called out, "God, I've always been very
religious. How could you let this happen to
me?" God answered, "To tell you the truth, I
didn't recognize you."

NATIONALITY

☐

_____'s grandfather came from
(Name)

_____ many years ago. He didn't
(Name of Country)

know English, but he managed to make a

fortune with just three words—"stick 'em up."

☐

_____ is an old friend of mine, and I just
(Name)

want you to know _____ has done a great
(he/she)

deal for the _____ people *just by not*
(Nationality)

being one.

☐

_____ loves the _____ people. A(n)
(Name)   (Nationality)

_____ family saved _____ life
(Nationality)   (his/her)

during the war by hiding _____ in their
(him/her)

basement. It was in San Francisco.

☐

Do you know the difference between the

Italian Mafia and the _____ Mafia?
(Nationality)

The Italian Mafia makes you an offer you

can't refuse, and the _____ Mafia
(Nationality)

makes you an offer you can't understand.

NONBELIEVER

☐

_____ once belonged to a religious cult
(Name)

called "Jemima's Witnesses." They wor-

shipped stacks of pancakes.

☐

_____ once wanted to become an atheist
(Name)

but soon dropped the idea—no holidays.

☐

Once _____ was very ill and almost
(Name)

didn't make it. A minister urged _____ to
(him/her)

renounce the devil. _____ said, "At a time
(Name)

like this, I'm not about to start making enemies."

☐

_____ recently started reading the Bible.
(Name)

_____ was pleased to find St. Paul men-
(He/She)

tioned several times but was puzzled that

there wasn't anything written about

Minneapolis.

PROTESTANT

❏

_____ and _____ _____ are
(Name)   (his/her) (wife/husband)
good Baptists, so they never make love

standing up. They don't want God to think

they're dancing.

❏

_____ is a WASP and proud of it. They
(Name)
say that God created WASPs so there'd be

someone to pay the full retail price.

❏

_____ told me what Baptists do after
(Name)
sex—apologize for any pleasure that might

have been experienced.

❏

_____ is a Lutheran. (You know, that's a
(Name)
person who has an uneasy feeling that some-

one, somewhere, is having a good time.)

Well, _____ went to a comedy show last
(he/she)
week and told me _____ _almost_ laughed.
(he/she)

Sex Life

DIRTY-MINDED

HORNY

❏

I asked _____ if _____ thought sex was
      (Name)   (he/she)
dirty. _____ responded, "Only if you do it
    (Name)
right."

❏

The doctor told _____ to cut down _____
        (Name)   (his/her)
sex life by half. _____ asked the doctor,
        (Name)
"Which half? The part I think about—or the

part I talk about?"

❏

_____ was asked to be the centerfold in
 (Name)
a dirty magazine, but _____ backed out at
           (he/she)
the last minute when _____ discovered
        (he/she)
where they were going to put the staples.

❏

The doctor recently told _____ that _____
          (Name)   (he/she)
should have _____ sex life lowered. Right
      (his/her)
now, it's all in _____ head.
        (his/her)

❏

I'll never forget the night I first met _____ .
            (Name)
She was standing on a street corner when

she spotted me and said, "Hey, Sailor! Buy

me a drink?"

❏

I overheard _____ bragging about
        (Name)
getting her purse stolen the other day. She

said it was the most attention she'd had from

a man in years.

❏

_____ considers sex a "misdemeanor."
 (Name)
_____ says, "The more I miss, de meaner
(He/She)
I get."

❏

Sex is one of _____'s favorite things in
        (Name)
life—it's right up there with glazed dough-

nuts.

HORNY

☐

_____ once went with a _____ who
(Name)   (girl/guy)
was a "ten and a half." That's a ten who
doesn't get headaches.

☐

_____ doesn't believe in having sex over
(Name)
fifty-five. _____ says it's best to pull over
(He/She)
to the side of the road.

☐

You know what _____ says after sex?
(Name)
"Are you guys all on the same team?"

☐

_____ was doing the lambada while two
(Name)
dogs looked on. The collie said, "What are
those people doing?" The German Shepherd
replied, "I don't know, but if *we* were doing
it, they'd throw a bucket of water on us."

IMPOTENT/INEPT

☐

What a lover that _____ is. Sometimes
(Name)
_____ _____ has to throw cold
(his/her) (wife/husband)
water on _____ when they're making
(him/her)
love—to wake _____ up.
(him/her)

☐

_____ 's _____ , _____ ,
(Name)   (wife/husband)   (Name of spouse)
used to be a telephone operator. So
whenever they make love, _____
(Name of spouse)
announces, "Your three minutes are up."

☐

Let's talk about _____'s love life. Last
(Name)
week _____ told _____ _____
(he/she)   (his/her) (wife/husband)
_____ would like to be on the bottom for a
(he/she)
change. So _____ got _____ a bunk bed.
(she/he)   (him/her)

☐

The first time _____ ever had sex,
(Name)
_____ whispered into _____ partner's
(he/she)   (his/her)
ear, "I love you, terribly." _____ partner
(His/Her)
whispered back, "You sure do."

IMPOTENT/INEPT

☐

As you know, we're in the middle of a sexual revolution. _____ says that it's just _____ luck to be out of ammunition.
(Name)   (his/her)

☐

_____ 's _____ recently filled out
(Name)   (wife/husband)
an application for a new job. In the space for "Sex," she wrote: "Occasionally."

☐

Once upon a time, _____ 's minister
(Name)
asked him: "Is an hour of pleasure worth a lifetime of shame?" And _____ answered:
(Name)
"How do you make it last an hour?"

☐

_____ and his wife are a perfect couple.
(Name)
She's positively electrifying, and he's out of batteries.

☐

_____ and _____ _____ sleep
(Name)   (his/her)   (wife/husband)
on a waterbed. _____ _____ refers
(His/Her)   (wife/husband)
to it as "the Dead Sea."

☐

But enough about _____ 's sex life.
(Name)
What's past is past.

☐

_____ called _____ _____
(Name)   (his/her)   (wife/husband)
yesterday and said, "Honey, I've been thinking about the last time we made love. I can't wait to see you. _____ 's
(Name)
_____ answered, "Who *is* this?"
(wife/husband)

☐

A marriage counselor asked _____ if
(Name)
_____ and _____ partner have mutual
(he/she)   (his/her)
climax, and _____ answered, "No, we
(he/she)
have New York Life."

KINKY

❑

_____ is the only man I know who can
(Name)
get turned on by undressing in front of his

Princess phone.

❑

_____ was born on a farm a long way
(Name)
from here—where men are men, and sheep

are nervous.

❑

_____ is a little depressed. Last week,
(Name)

_____ inflatable _____ sprang
(his/her)   (girlfriend/boyfriend)
a leak.

❑

_____ says _____ hung up last week
(Name)   (he/she)
in the middle of an obscene phone call—

_____ couldn't think of any more to say.
(he/she)

❑

_____ explained the difference between
(Name)
weird sex and kinky sex. Weird sex is when

you use a feather. Kinky sex is when you use

the whole chicken.

❑

_____'s parents were shocked when
(Name)
they found out that _____ had been
(he/she)
playing doctor with a _____ who lived
(girl/boy)
next door. _____ _____ wasn't too
(His/Her)   (wife/husband)
happy about it either.

❑

I was in the locker room the other day with

_____ and noticed _____ was
(Name)   (he/she)
wearing _____. I asked when
(panties/jockey shorts)
_____ started wearing _____
(he/she)   (women's/men's)
underwear, and _____ said ever since
(he/she)
_____ _____ found them in the
(his/her)   (wife/husband)
glove compartment.

KINKY

❏

A few years ago _____ was out of town
        (Name)
at a convention. When I called _____ hotel
                              (his/her)
room, I heard a loud noise in the back-

ground. I asked _____ , "What's that
              (Name)
racket?" _____ replied, "A _____
        (He/She)   (woman/man)
is pounding on my door." "Why don't you let

_____ in?" I asked. _____ answered,
(her/him)   (Name)
" _____ trying to get *out*."
 (He's/She's)

❏

Sometimes _____ talks to _____
         (Name)   (his/her)
_____ when _____ makes love—if
(wife/husband)   (he/she)
there's a phone handy.

❏

When _____ was a senior in high school,
     (Name)
_____ principal asked, "Which college
(his/her)
are you going to?" _____ responded,
                  (Name)
"Either Harvard or Radcliffe—depending on

how my sex change operation turns out."

❏

Early in their marriage, _____ and
                        (Name)
_____ _____ made an agreement
(his/her) (wife/husband)
to go out once a week for a romantic

candlelight dinner. _____ goes out
                   (Name)
Tuesdays and _____ _____ goes out
            (his/her) (wife/husband)
Thursdays.

❏

I have an announcement: Our good friend,

_____ just became the father of a seven-
(Name)
pound baby boy this morning. How about a

nice hand for the new father.

(Wait for applause.)

If his wife ever finds out, she'll kill him.

NAIVE

❑

A good-looking _____ stopped _____
(girl/guy)   (Name)
on the street and told _____ _____ would
                       (him/her) (she/he)
do anything for fifty dollars. So, _____ took
                                    (Name)
_____ home and said: "Paint my house."
(her/him)

❑

A friend told _____ that _____ was
             (Name)   (he/she)
having an affair, and _____ replied,
                       (Name)
"Who's catering it?"

❑

The first time _____ went on a car-date,
               (Name)
_____ date asked _____ , "Do you
(his/her)   (him/her)
want to go in the back seat?" "Nothing

doing," _____ replied. "I want to stay up
         (he/she)
here with you."

❑

_____ was so naive as a teenager that
(Name)
_____ would sneak behind the barn and
(he/she)
do *nothing.*

❑

_____ recently stayed in a hotel where
(Name)
the people in the next room were honey-

mooners. _____ said they kept _____
          (Name)   (him/her)
awake all night long eating candy bars—at

least _____ thought they were, because
      (he/she)
_____ could hear the woman moaning,
(he/she)
"Oh Henry! Oh Henry!"

Endings

COMEBACKS

☐

_____, is your speech over, or can I
(Name)
finish my nap?

☐

I might not agree with what you said,

_____, but I'll always defend your right
(Name)
to make a fool of yourself.

☐

_____, why don't you sit down and rest
(Name)
your brains.

☐

_____, you've always been a big help to
(Name)
people. But so has Ex-Lax.

☐

_____, if they ever put a price on your
(Name)
head—take it!

☐

_____, you can brighten up a room—
(Name)
just by leaving it.

☐

I never forget a face—but in your case,

_____, I'll make an exception.
(Name)

☐

_____, you're one of a kind. There's no
(Name)
one else exactly like you—thank God!

CLOSING REMARKS

❑

In conclusion, _____ is very difficult to
(Name)
describe. I guess you might say _____ has
(he/she)
that certain nothing.

❑

_____, you sure know how to make
(Name)
people happy. All you have to do is leave
the room.

❑

Well, _____, I really do think the world of
(Name)
you. Of course, you know the shape the
world is in these days.

❑

_____, I like you. I really do—as long as
(Name)
you're buying the drinks.

❑

Actually, _____, you're great. I think all
(Name)
your friends are wrong.

❑

One thing I have to admit is _____ grows
(Name)
on you—sort of like a fungus.

❑

_____, you're a person who's hard to
(Name)
forget. But the same can be said of Saddam
Hussein.

❑

Remember, _____—if you ever need a
(Name)
friend, buy a dog.

The Best Baby Shower Book

by Courtney Cooke

Finally, a complete guide for planning baby showers that's chock-full of helpful hints, recipes, decorating ideas, and activities that are fun without being juvenile.

Order # 1239

The Best Wedding Shower Book

by Courtney Cooke

The complete guide for planning wedding showers. Contains time- and money-saving ideas for decorating, food, innovative gifts, and fun, creative games.

Order # 6059

The Best Party Book

by Penny Warner

Over 1,000 creative ideas for planning birthdays, anniversaries, graduation
parties, holiday parties, plus Super Bowl and Academy Awards parties.

Order # 6089

Order Form

Qty.	Title	Author	Order No.	Unit Cost	Total
	Best Baby Shower Book, The	Cooke, C.	1239	$6.00	
	Best Party Book, The	Warner, P.	6089	$7.00	
	Best Wedding Shower Book, The	Cooke, C.	6059	$6.00	
	Dads Say the Dumbest Things!	Lansky/Jones	4220	$6.00	
	Grandma Knows Best	McBride, M.	4009	$5.00	
	How To Survive Your 40th Birthday	Dodds, B.	4260	$5.00	
	Italian Without Words	Cangelosi/Carpini	5100	$4.95	
	Kids Pick the Funniest Poems	Lansky, B.	2410	$13.00	
	Moms Say the Funniest Things!	Lansky, B.	4280	$6.00	
	Mother Murphy's Law	Lansky, B.	1149	$4.50	
	Mother Murphy's Law 2	Lansky, B.	4010	$4.50	
	World's Funniest Roast Jokes	Stangland, R.	4030	$6.00	
				Subtotal	
			Shipping and Handling (see below)		
			MN residents add 6.5% sales tax		
				Total	

YES! Please send me the books indicated above. Add $1.50 shipping and handling for the first book and 50¢ for each additional book. Add $2.00 to total for books shipped to Canada. Overseas postage will be billed. Allow up to 4 weeks for delivery. Send check or money order payable to Meadowbrook Press. No cash or C.O.D's, please. Prices subject to change without notice. **Quantity discounts available upon request.**

Send book(s) to:

Name _____ Address _____

City _____ State _____ Zip _____

Telephone (_____)_____ P.O. number (if necessary) _____

Payment via: ☐ Check or money order payable to Meadowbrook Press (No cash or C.O.D.'s, please)

Amt. enclosed $_____ ☐ Visa (for orders over $10.00 only.) ☐ MasterCard (for orders over $10.00 only.)

Account # _____ Signature _____ Exp. Date _____

A *FREE* Meadowbrook Press catalog is available upon request.
You can also phone us for orders of $10.00 or more at 1-800-338-2232.

Mail to: Meadowbrook, Inc.
18318 Minnetonka Boulevard, Deephaven, MN 55391

(612) 473-5400　　　　Toll-Free 1-800-338-2232　　　　Fax (612) 475-0736